OCT 15 2013

2012 TOP COUNTRY HITS 2013

782.4216

ISBN 978-1-4803-3798-5

HAL•LEONARD®
CORPORATION
7777 W. BLUEMOUND RD. P.O. BOX 13819 MILWAUKEE, WI 53213

Visit Hal Leonard Online at
www.halleonard.com

BEER MONEY

Words and Music by TROY VERGES,
BLAIR DALY and KIP MOORE

BETTER DIG TWO

Words and Music by SHANE McANALLY,
BRANDY CLARK and TREVOR ROSEN

Moderately

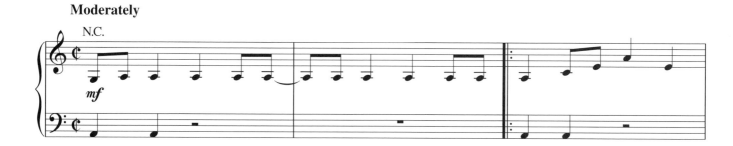

I told you on the day we wed I was gon-na love you till I's dead.

Made you wait till our wed-ding night. That's the

BEGIN AGAIN

Words and Music by
TAYLOR SWIFT

Moderately

Took a deep breath in the mir - ror.

He did - n't like it when I wore high heels, but I_____ do.

And ___ we walked down the block ___ to my car

COME WAKE ME UP

Words and Music by SEAN McCONNELL,
JOHAN FRANSSON, TIM LARSSON
and TOBIAS LUNDGREN

EVERY STORM
(Runs Out of Rain)

Words and Music by MATT WARREN,
HILLARY LINDSEY and GARY ALLAN

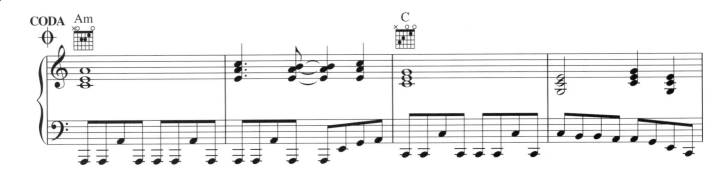

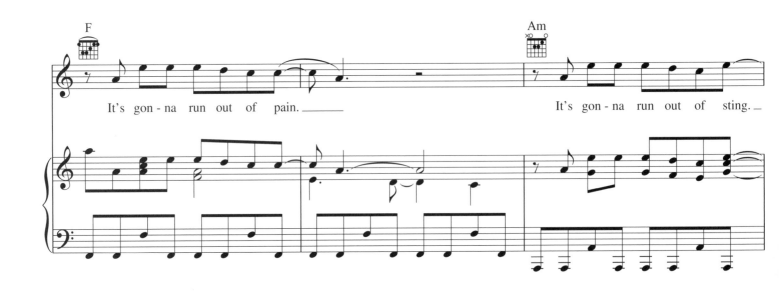

FASTEST GIRL IN TOWN

Words and Music by MIRANDA LAMBERT
and ANGALEENA PRESLEY

*Recorded a half step lower.

HARD TO LOVE

Words and Music by BEN GLOVER,
BILLY MONTANA and JOHN OZIER

KISS TOMORROW GOODBYE

Words and Music by LUKE BRYAN,
JEFF STEVENS and SHANE McANALLY

THE ONE THAT GOT AWAY

Words and Music by JOSHUA OWEN,
DALLAS DAVIDSON and JIMMY RITCHEY

OVER YOU

Words and Music by MIRANDA LAMBERT
and BLAKE SHELTON

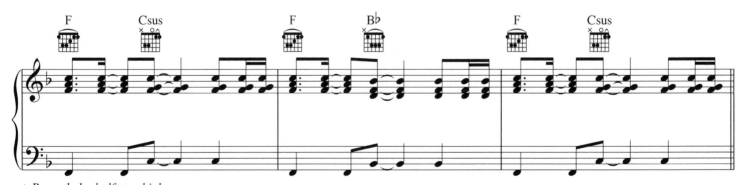

* *Recorded a half step higher.*

RED

Words and Music by
TAYLOR SWIFT

TIL MY LAST DAY

Words and Music by JEREMY STOVER,
JUSTIN MOORE and BRIAN MAHER

WANTED

Words and Music by HUNTER HAYES
and TROY VERGES

WE ARE NEVER EVER GETTING BACK TOGETHER

Words and Music by TAYLOR SWIFT,
SHELLBACK and MAX MARTIN

Moderately

I re-mem-ber when we broke _ up, the first time, say-in' this is it, I've had e-nough. But 'cause like we

had-n't seen each oth-er in a month when you said you need-ed space. What?

TAKE A LITTLE RIDE

Words and Music by DYLAN ALTMAN,
JAMES McCORMICK and RODNEY CLAWSON